OBJECT LESSONS
FOR
CHILDREN

Also Usable as Story Sermons, Chalk, Picture, Puppet, or Bedtime Stories

Luther Cross

BAKER BOOK HOUSE
Grand Rapids, Michigan

ISBN: 0-8010-2315-7

First printing, December 1967
Second printing, August 1969
Third printing, February 1971
Fourth printing, August 1972
Fifth printing, December 1973

Printed in the United States of America

INTRODUCTION

It was at vacation Bible school, as a high school student, that I heard and saw my first object lesson. I had been in church all of my life, but here was something that was a breed apart from all the lessons I had heard before. The entire group was spellbound. I saw in the object lesson a packaged form of "instant attention."

If a children's show on television should ever be foolish enough to present a lecture without story or visual display in it, it would be tuned off by children, and would soon be off the air. The same fate awaits the religious teacher who attempts to teach with merely a lecture. He is instantly tuned out of the mind of the child who fidgets in front of him. A children's sermon should be a (1) story with an (2) object lesson or visual display, and it should be (3) related to a child's experience. In this day of television anything less than this is obsolete.

There is nothing new about this. Our Savior, the greatest teacher of all, used these three methods. I like to imagine that he pointed to a wheat field or a flock of sheep and goats or some other object as he spoke. If not, the objects that he mentioned in his parables and lessons were easily visualized in the imagination. His object lessons included barns, candles, coins, a pearl, leaven, fish, sheep, goats, crops, salt, flash floods, bread, wine, towers, and the like.

This is an exciting way to teach, and one that will bring real satisfaction to hearer-viewer and speaker-exhibitor alike.

This book is a continuation of the approach used in its sister volume, *Story Sermons for Children*. The two books between them cover the major events of the church year and supplement each other in the doctrines covered.

CONTENTS

OBJECT LESSONS

CHILDREN'S SERMON TECHNIQUES

OBJECT LESSONS

Well done, good and faithful servant.
—Matthew 25:21

1. That Certain Something

There was a little boy who had something wrong with his throat so that he could not talk. Everybody called him Shadow, because he was always around but nobody ever noticed him. Shadow attended church school for ten years without missing. He attended junior youth fellowship for four years without missing. However everyone thought he was useless, because he was so shy that he sat by himself in a corner and never helped with a thing. He even came to youth fellowship the day he fell out of a tree and broke his arm and had a terrible headache. The Sunday they had the bad snow storm, he waded through a foot and a half of snow, and was the only person at youth fellowship besides the advisor.

While Shadow was still very young, he died and went to be with God in heaven. Shadow's guardian angel was there to welcome him when he arrived. In heaven Shadow saw that they were making plans for a great celebration. His guardian angel told him that they were planning a reception for one of the finest Christians in the world. All the angels were getting lined up to sing a mighty chorus of praise. There was to be a great parade and there was a glorious golden chair that the Christian hero was to ride in.

Shadow began to cry. "How I wish I could have done something wonderful for Jesus, but I could not sing, I could not answer my church school teacher's questions, I could not help in church in any way. I was completely useless, like a bump on a log."

Shadow longed to see the great Christian hero. He also longed to sit in the wonderful golden chair for just a minute.

"Do you mind if I sit in the hero's chair for just a minute before he comes?" Shadow asked his guardian angel.

With the angels permission, Shadow climbed up into the beautiful chair.

"When do you think the hero will come?' Shadow asked his angel.

"The hero is sitting in the golden chair this very minute," smiled the angel.

"Why there's nobody in the chair but me!" exclaimed Shadow.

"Of course, you are the great hero," answered the angel. "You have that certain something."

"What certain something?" wondered Shadow.

The angel continued, "There were twenty children in your junior youth fellowship, but it would have died without the eight who had that certain something. There were one hundred and fifty members in your church but it would have died without the forty people who had that certain something."

"What certain something?" broke in Shadow.

The angel continued, "There have been many great Christians, great missionaries, church leaders, but everybody who has really been of service to Jesus has had that certain something. Without them God's church could not exist. Without that certain something people are useless for God. Shadow, you are a great hero, a soldier for God!"

"Aren't you going to tell me what that certain something is?" demanded Shadow.

"God is spelling it out in the sky right now!" replied the angel.

With great fiery letters in all the colors of the rainbow, God wrote the letters. So big and glorious they were that they filled the entire heavens with light as far as the eye could see in every direction. He wrote the letters one by one: "F" . . . "A" . . . "I" . . . "T" . . . "H" . . . "F" . . . "U" . . . "L".

"That is it," said the angel. "You were faithful."

✓ *Object Lesson Application*

Display a cutout of a boy, cut from a mail order catalogue. Remark that, although the boy was very small, he had a giant soul. Here hold up a large, white paper heart, which is much bigger than the boy. Remark that the boy had made the soul great by the way he had served God on earth. When the secret of Shadow's greatness is revealed in the

8

story, turn the heart around to show the word, "Faithful," on its reverse.

Picture or Chalk Talk Application

The sign overhead in the illustration is made by drawing the word, "Faithful" with various bright chalk colors, on the page underneath that of your picture. A long flap of the top drawing page is lightly cut with a razor, along the area indicated by the dotted lines. This is so you can peal this flap of paper away at the appropriate time, to show the word "Faithful." Attach the two pages of your drawing paper together in back of the lower slit, with a non-wrinkling adhesive such as rubber cement or liquid plastic. A few pieces of scotch tape or masking tape will also serve the purpose.

First draw Shadow on his throne. When the word, "Faithful," is revealed in the heavens, reveal your word, "Faithful," pulling the flap back to reveal the letters one by one as indicated in the story. Now extend Shadow's sad mouth into a smile, as indicated by the face to the left of Shadow's in the drawing. This face indicates the change and is not to be drawn as an additional face to the side.

Puppet Talk Application

Present the same as indicated in the object lesson application, but substituting a hand puppet, for the cutout of a boy.

Love your enemies and pray for those
who persecute you.—Matthew 5:44

2. The Girl Who Swallowed an Egg Beater

There was a little girl named Madeline Gladys Glenn, except everybody called her "Mad' for short. She was very unusual. Instead of sneezing out, like this, "Kachooo"; she sneezed in, like this, "aaakooo." (Inhale a sneeze.)

Once when Mad was licking the egg beater after her mother made a cake, she gave a great big, inside-out sneeze and swallowed the egg beater. Having an egg beater inside never bothered Mad a bit, except when people teased her, then it started beating inside of her, and made her all stirred up and angry. Everytime the boys teased her she became angry, so they teased her every time they saw her.

When the boys saw Mad they would yell, "Mad is a crybaby. Mad is a crybaby. Mad is a crybaby."

Immediately Mad would get angry, the egg beater inside her would start to churn, her face would get red, and she would start to cry. She would chase the boys and throw sticks at them. She could not run very fast and she could not hit anything with a stick, so the boys enjoyed this a great deal. They would keep just out of reach and yell and laugh at her. Poor little Mad.

One day in church school the teacher told the children how mean people beat Jesus and nailed him to a cross, but still he loved them just the same and asked God to forgive them. Suddenly Mad realized that it is not what people do to you on the outside that makes you unhappy, but whether or not you stay sweet on the inside. If people are mean to you and you just love them back, what they do will not make you feel mean inside. Mad made up her mind that no matter what the boys said to hurt her on the outside, she would not start hating them and make her egg beater stir her up on the inside.

After church school, Mad ran out to where the naughty boys were. Immediately they started to chant, "Mad is a crybaby." Mad looked at the boys and tried to love them. She prayed for them. She was surprised to find that their name calling did not bother her at all. The more they called her names, the more she smiled. The boys yelled until their faces got red and their voices got hoarse, but still Mad just smiled. After that the boys stopped calling her names because it was no longer any fun.

Mad had learned that smart people do not let their egg beaters get turned on no matter what happens on the outside. Soon Madeline Gladys Glenn got a new nickname. They started calling her "Glad" for short.

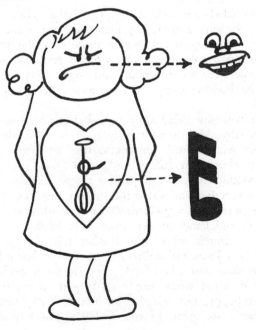

Object Lesson Application

Paste a picture of a small girl (one you have drawn or cut from a magazine) onto the side of a glass full of vinegar on top of a tray. Tell how it made Mad angry on the inside when people were unkind to the outside of her. Liken the name calling and unkindness, on the outside, to someone beating against one's outside. Demonstrate this by beating against the glass, which represents Mad, with a spoon. Show how Mad's anger on the inside of her got her stirred up, by stirring a heaping tablespoon of baking soda into the vinegar. Mad's anger will then "boil over" onto the tray. When Mad reforms, again beat on her outside with a spoon, but this time put a third spoon, which has a red heart taped on its bowl, into the glass. The heart represents her love for her enemies. With love on the inside, their taunts do not bother her at all.

Picture or Chalk Talk Application

Draw Mad as illustrated. The objects to her side, indicate modifications that are to be made in the girl, and are not of course, separate drawings to be made to the side of Mad. When Mad reforms, the egg beater is changed into a note of joy, by blacking over it. Her frown is changed into a smile in this manner: first add the open mouthed smile so that its corners meet at either end of the frowning mouth. Next draw a round nose above the frowning mouth. The thick lines of this nose cover up the two eye pupils. The frowning lines of the eyebrows are expanded into half circle shaped eyes. A new set of pupils is added into the new eyes.

Object Talk Application

Use a two-faced light bulb hand puppet where the face changes into a smile when the light comes on. (Pages 94-95.) Develop this application the same as is done with the object lesson application. Beat against the side of the puppet with a spoon. Discover that the reason for the puppet's anger at this treatment is a spoon which is stirring it up on the inside. Remove a second spoon from inside the puppet's costume. When Mad reforms, place a heart, representing love, inside of her costume. Beat on her with the spoon from the outside, but this time the puppet responds with smiles. (Manipulate the puppet to make it smile.)

12

Do not be overcome by evil, but overcome evil with good.—Romans 12:21

3. Empty Minds

"Oh dear! I just know something bad will happen," coo cooed the cuckoo clock on the wall. "I just know it. There are little Tom and Tammy with nothing to do. Their minds are empty. An idle mind is the devil's workshop. They will certainly think up something bad to do. It's idle children like this that join gangs and rob stores, or get into fights. Oh, dear."

Sure enough, Tom and Tammy both had empty minds. They wailed, "I don't know what to do."

By the time Mother came back home, Tammy had given Tom a haircut, a can of red paint had been spilled on the new living room carpet, and a vase had been broken.

"I just don't know what to do with these children," Mother screamed. "I have tried spanking them. I have tried talking to them. I have tried everything, but still they get into trouble."

Just then the door of the cuckoo clock opened. The little bird came out, cleared its throat, and cooed in its politest manner, "May I say something."

"Certainly not," frowned Mother. "No cuckoo clock can tell me anything."

"You are a coo coo mother," replied the clock.

"What would you do with the children then?" demanded Mother.

The bird answered, "They get into trouble because they don't know what to do with themselves. Instead of punishing them, give them something good to do and they will keep out of trouble. As it says in the Bible, "Do not be covercome by evil, but overcome evil with good."

13

By the next week Tom was working on his God and Country Award for Scouts and Tammy had joined the Four-H Club. When Mother left them alone one afternoon she returned to find Tom busy memorizing the Twenty-third Psalm, and Tammy making cookies to take to a lonesome old woman who lived down the street. They had been too busy doing good to get into trouble.

Just then the clock opened its door and the bird hollered out, "smart smart, smart smart, smart smart."

"Why don't you say 'coo coo' like you are supposed to?" asked Mommy.

"You aren't coo coo anymore," said the bird.

Object Lesson Application

Use the glass, with the girl on the outside, that you have prepared for the object lesson in the previous story sermon. Show that the girl is susceptible to trouble by taking a box or glass labelled, "trouble," and pouring a load of corks from this container into the empty glass representing the girl. The emptiness of the glass represents the fact that her mind was empty, or without useful occupation. Take a third container full of water, and labeled, "Good things," (to do); and pour this into the glass now full of corks. Putting the water into the glass will make the corks overflow out of it (with the help of your hand to brush off the bottom layer and onto a tray underneath. This represents the fact that a busy mind does not have room for evil temptations. The glass representing the girl has a girl's picture on one side, and is transparent on the back, so the congregation can see the load of corks being displaced by the water.

Picture or Chalk Talk Application

Draw the boy with the empty head as illustrated. Next add the "evil temptation" knocking on the empty head for admittance. The light bulb shown is not a part of the chalk drawing but is either a cardboard cut-out, or a real light bulb, labeled, "Good Thoughts." Sticky-side-out circlets of masking tape will stick onto the empty brain, thus filling it, so the temptation cannot enter. Carry out this application along the lines suggested in the object lesson application above.

For a special effect it is possible to get a light bulb from a magic trick supply house that will light up without any electrical cord. You will need to tape a piece of wire across the terminals to make the circuit complete.

Puppet Talk Application

Use a light bulb puppet without the bulb in the socket. (See pages

14

93-96.) Use paper clips to fasten a cardboard strip onto the inside of the paper head cylinder. The strip will extend down into the hand holding the puppet, where the third and fourth fingers will hold it (and the head) in place. You now have a hollow head which can be tilted to show that it is empty. This application will be developed the same as the picture talk application. First put something that represents evil into the empty head and then displace it with something that represents good. Possible items for this are a wad of black paper and a wad of white paper, or a paper cutout of a devil and a paper heart, or a bottle labeled, "poisonous thoughts," and a small scripture portion or a small pamphlet labeled, "Holy Bible."

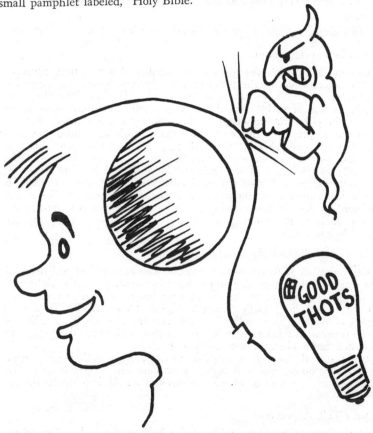

Follow me, and I will make you fishers
of men.

—Matthew 4:19

1/25/76

4. A Fisher of Men

There was a picture in the church school classroom that little Martin loved very much. It showed Jesus talking to his disciples. His arm was around one, a man wearing a brown robe. Jesus was looking at his disciples with a burning gaze and they looked back at him steadfastly. He was sending them out to preach and win other people to a love of God and everlasting life. Beneath the picture were the words, "I will make you fishers of men."

Martin thought to himself, "If only I could have been one of those disciples. How wonderful it would have been to have Jesus send me out to win other people to him. This would be more wonderful than going in a rocket to the moon, or being President of the United States, or hitting sixty-two home runs in the major leagues."

Just then the minister walked in the room and asked who was the new boy sitting next to Martin. Nobody in the whole room knew except the boy himself and Martin.

"His name is James," said Martin, "He's new in town, I invited him to go to church school with me."

Martin was surprised at what the minister said next.

"This is wonderful," he said. "I am proud of you Martin. I probably could not have persuaded him to come and my elders probably could not have done it. It took a boy like you to persuade a friend to come. This is the way the church grows, when people like you bring their friends. I am sure that Jesus is proud of you, too."

Martin looked at the picture of Jesus again. In his imagination, the face of the man in the brown robe became Martin's own face. Yes, even now, Martin was a fisher of men for Jesus.

Object Lesson Application

1. Display a picture of Christ sending out his disciples to preach.

A suitable picture would be, "Go Forth and Preach" by Burnand, obtainable for 15c plus 20c postage and handling, size 8″ x 10″, color, from W. A. Wilde Co., 10 Huron Drive, Natick, Massachusetts.

2. An alternate approach is to display a stick with a red cross taped to it. The stick has a string on it in the fashion of a crude fishing pole. On the other end of the string is a cutout of a man, cut out of a mail order catalog. This device represents the symbolic tool of a person who is fishing for men to win them to Christ.

Picture or Chalk Talk Application

Draw as illustrated. The boy's head, at one side, is not a part of the chalk drawing. This is a cutout of a boy's head obtained from a magazine, or one which you have drawn. It can be in color in contrast with the black and white lines of the chalk drawing. At the proper time in the story, the cutout, representing Martin, is fastened over the face of the disciple. A sticky-side-out circlet of scotch tape on the back of the cutout is used.

Puppet Talk Application

Use a hand puppet and the objects and method indicated in the second object lesson application. The puppet shows his gimmicked fishing rod to the sermonizer, and expresses a desire to be a fisher of men, and the sermonizer tells the puppet the story of Martin. (See pages 93ff. for methods of having the puppet "talk.")

5. The Girl Who Acted Like a Cactus

Little Kitty never thought about anyone but herself. As with most very selfish people, it was very easy for her to get her feelings hurt. She got them hurt when people intended no harm at all.

Once after Kitty had been playing at Sally Jane's house, she put on her coat and opened the door to leave.

"Goodbye," said Sally Jane politely.

Kitty got her feelings hurt. "You're just saying 'goodbye' to make me leave sooner. I hate you," said Kitty.

She slapped Sally Jane's face. Poor Sally Jane had meant no harm.

Another time, Kitty entered church school just as George was telling the other children something funny he saw on television. They all laughed. Kitty thought they were laughing at her so she slapped George. Of course, George had not been talking about her at all.

Everybody began to keep away from Kitty, as they never knew when she would get her feelings hurt. She got her feelings hurt so often that her face started to turn green. Pretty soon sharp thorns started to grow out all over her face and body. She was turning into a cactus plant. A cactus is a lonely plant that lives out in the desert with thorns on it to keep people away.

Finally Kitty's parents went to an orphanage and adopted the most crippled child they could find for Kitty to take care of. They knew that if Kitty did not learn to think about somebody besides herself, she would continue getting her feelings hurt and being lonely all of her life. I certainy hope Kitty gets over getting her feelings hurt. Nobody wants to be around a person who behaves like a prickly cactus.

18

Object Lesson Application

Display a cactus plant or a paper cutout of one made of green construction paper and copied from our illustration, face and all.

Picture or Chalk Talk Application

Draw as illustrated.

Puppet Talk Application

Make a cactus glove puppet. (See pages 96-97.)

Forgive us our debts, As we also have
forgiven our debtors.—Matthew 6:12

Forgiveness

august 3, 1975

6.   Christine
Forgives

Christine cried for half an hour. She was very bitter toward Frog
Timmons, the neighborhood bully. She had wanted a cocker spaniel
with all of her heart for many years and recently she had received
her very own little puppy for her birthday. A few nights ago the
puppy did not return home and she found that Frog had killed it
with his father's shotgun. How Christine wished she were a boy
and bigger than Frog so she could bloody his nose, blacken his eyes,
and beat him to a pulp. That night when Christine knelt by her
bed to say her prayers, she tried to say, "Dear God, please make
Frog get sick!" but she knew it would not be right to ask God to
do something like this.

She was so angry, she could not say her prayers at all. Usually
she was very happy when she said her prayers. God seemed like a
warm, wonderful Friend to her, but now he seemed far away. She
tried to say the Lord's Prayer, but when she got to the part, "Forgive us our debts, as we forgive our debtors," she knew she could
not say that. She remembered how the sixth chapter of Matthew,
where the Lord's Prayer is found, also has the words, "If you do
not forgive men their trespasses, neither will your Father forgive
your trespasses." This made Christine feel uncomfortable. It had
always made her feel good before, to ask God to forgive her for
the times she had been naughty during the day.

For the next two days Christine's anger at Frog would often
come back to her. It would make her feel mean and unhappy
inside and sometimes give her headaches. At the end of the second
day, Christine made up her mind that she wanted to be able to
talk to God again. She knelt by her bed and prayed, "Dear God, I

20

forgive Frog. Please bless him. He must be unhappy because he does such mean things. Please help him learn to be good."

How good Christine felt. A great load seemed to tumble off of her heart. Christine asked her brother who attended college if she could have one of his baseball mitts, that he no longer used; and she gave the mitt to Frog.

"What did you want to do that for?" asked her brother. "Doing nice things for Frog won't make him get better."

"Well, even if it doesn't help Frog," smiled Christine, "it has helped me feel better already."

Object Lesson Application

In telling the story, hold up a picture of Christ, or a silhouette-cutout of a picture, or a paper cross, to represent him. This shows that Christine is close to Christ. When Christine gets a load of hate in her heart, hold up a black paper cloud in front of Christ, to show that she has lost the joy of her close fellowship. Remove the cloud at the appropriate time.

Picture or Chalk Talk Application

Draw as illustrated, except that Christine is shown to have just a straight line for a mouth, indicating a neutral expression. When Christine comes close to Christ again, extend her mouth upward into the smile shown in the illustration.

Puppet Talk Application

Use a hand puppet and the objects indicated in the object lesson application. The puppet is cast in the role of Christine, and the cloud is shown to obscure her vision of Christ.

Use of a two faced or expression changing light bulb puppet is optional. (See pages 94-95.)

Let us consider how to stir up one another to love and to good works.
—Hebrews 10:24

7. Butch's Meanness

Butch always had a frown on his face. There seemed to be a
black cloud of meanness floating around his head. He was always
hitting the little kindergarten children like Laurie. He was always
getting into fights. The third grade teacher was always sending him
to the principal's office. He wore dirty clothes that were several
sizes too large for him, and only wore one ragged sweater during
the coldest days of winter.

One day the police caught him breaking into a store. The judge
at Children's Court decided that Butch's uncle was not taking the
right care of him, and he would have to live somewhere else. Butch
had no place to go. Nobody wanted him.

How surprised Laurie was when she found out that her parents
felt that it was their Christian duty to adopt Butch.

"I'll just die when the other kids find out," wailed Laurie.

Mother replied, "The reason Butch has the cloud of meanness
around his head, is because he is a poor little boy who has been
starved for love. He can't love other people because he doesn't
know how. His heart is sick and broken. We've got to keep showing
him love and kindness till finally that broken heart is healed and
the cloud of meanness goes away."

Butch moved in. All he owned in the world were a few clothes
and a dirty, ragged teddy bear. He kept it in a box so nobody could
see that he had it, and he refused to let anyone touch the box. Many
times, when he was alone in his room, Laurie thought she heard
him talking to his teddy bear.

Butch was always very rude and bad mannered with his new

family. The more love they showed him, the worse he behaved. They thought his cloud of meanness would never go away. This kept up for almost a year until Laurie was hit by a car.

She was not hurt badly, but the doctor put her to bed at home anyway. Then she heard the screen door bang, and Butch's voice gasp, "Doc! is my sister dead?"

A little later she saw the door knob turn very slowly. She saw Butch's face peering in. His eyes were red. She knew it would embrassed him if she caught him crying so she pretended to be asleep. He tiptoed in. He came closer, and closer, and closer to her. Then he left. When he had gone she opened her eyes and she knew that the cloud of meanness had at last left Butch. There beside her on her pillow was a dirty, ragged teddy bear.

Object Lesson Application

Make a black cloud out of construction paper. The back side of the cloud is brown, made from a piece of construction paper pasted on. The brown side is painted to look like a teddy bear. The picture talk drawing shows a sample cloud and bear.

Show the appropriate sides of your cloud-bear at the proper times in the story.

Picture or Chalk Talk Application

Draw the boy as illustrated. Around him, in our illustration, are three objects which are not a part of your drawing. The face to one side depicts the changes to be made in Butch's expression at the close of the story. His mouth is extended on either side into a smile. Pupils are added on top of his frowning eyebrows, making them into the bottom eyelids. The eyes are altered to appear as shown. The gloom cloud is a cutout made in advance, with a teddy bear on the reverse side, according to instructions in the object lesson application. The gloom cloud is seen to rest over Butch's head, and at the proper time is reversed and re-applied to the drawing paper, so that the bear is visible. Sticky-side-out circlets of masking tape are used to hold the cloud-bear in place. It will not be necessary to heal the rift in Butch's heart as shown in the chalk drawing, although this can be done by drawing the heart initially in solid red, so that a stroke of red chalk can cover the rift.

Puppet Talk Application

Use a hand puppet with a cloud of gloom which is stuck to his forehead at first, and reversed to become a bear at the last. The presentation is like that suggested in the above applications. In addition a red heart with a black rift in it can be pinned in advance on the puppet's costume.

Love is not jealous.—I Corinthians 13:4

8. The Broken Dish

Mother asked Little Sister to feed the dog. Little Brother became very jealous. He wanted to help his mother feed the dog instead of having his sister do it. As sister carefully carried the bowl of dog food, Little Brother pushed her down. The bowl broke and gravy spilled all over Little Sister's new dress. Little Sister sat down and cried her heart out. Little Brother felt bad too and sat down beside her crying.

When Mother came, Little Brother said, "Why didn't you let me feed the dog? I would have done it."

"Because you helped Father rake the leaves this morning," said Mother. Father and I love both of you just the same, so we let you take turns helping us."

When suppertime came, Father started to carve the chicken when Mother cried, "No! no! Let me carve the chicken. I don't want Little Brother and Little Sister to love you more than me."

When bedtime came Mother started to read the children a story when Father yelled, "No! no! Let me read them a story. I don't want the children to love you more than me."

"Stop arguing this minute!" said Little Brother. "I love Daddy for cutting my meat and Mother for reading me stories. I love you both."

"They are just pretending. They are not really arguing," said Little Sister. "They are just showing us how silly we are when we argue about who's going to feed the dog. Father and Mother can't both cut the meat or read us stories at once so they take turns and that's the reason we have to take turns helping them."

Object Lesson Application

Display a large face. On one side it is green and on the other side it is white or flesh colored. Use two pieces of construction paper, pasted

26

together, to make this. The size should be the maximum possible obtained from the paper. The faces could either be circular, made with the use of a round dish or a compass, or oval, in which case symetry may be obtained by folding the paper in half lengthwise and cutting both sides at once. The green face is unhappy while the flesh colored one is gay. See page 70 for suggested features.

Use the appropriate sides of the face to tell the story and the folly of jealousy. The green face is a jealous one, of course. The happy face shows the joy of trusting in a parent's love.

Picture or Chalk Talk Application

Draw the two dark upside down hearts first, saying that the two children are loved equally by their parents. Make the hearts into the children as you tell of their jealousy. Add the large heart around them at the end, as you state that a child can trust in a parent's love, as it is big enough to include them all in it.

Puppet Talk Application

Develop as indicated in the object lesson application. Use a green light bulb puppet (see pages 93-96), showing the unhappy expression first, and flicking on the green light at the point in the story when the children cry. Turn the puppet around to its happy side during the last paragraph of the story.

9. Junior's Example

Daddy, Mother, Junior, and Sissy were riding home in the family car. It was way past lunch time and Junior was so hungry that he could hardly stand it.

"Hey stop!" he cried, "There's a place where we can eat and save my life."

Daddy replied, "That restaurant is really a gambling joint. If people saw us eat there, they would think that we weren't Christians."

"If we just took some sandwiches out, it wouldn't hurt anything," pleaded Junior.

"No, I don't want to do anything that might hurt someone else," said Daddy. "No matter who you are, there is always someone else who will be made better or worse by your example. Remember that, Son."

"I sure will, Dad. I wouldn't want to make anybody worse by something I did, and it would be a wonderful way to serve Jesus, if I could make somebody else better by my example. When I grow up, I'm going to be the finest man I can."

After lunch, Junior and his friend, Sonny were playing marbles. Little Sissy came out with some chipped marbles that she had found.

"Go away," commanded Junior. "Girls can't play marbles."

Sissy refused to leave.

Junior said, "If you don't go away, you little pest, I'm going to tell Mother on you."

Junior gave Sissy's hair a tug to emphasize his point, and into the house she went wailing.

28

The next day Junior was sitting in his tree house thinking about what a nuisance little sisters were, when he noticed the four-year-old boy next door playing marbles while his dog tried to lick his face.

The little boy yelled, "Go away Spot. Dogs can't play marbles. If you don't go away, you little pest, I'm going to tell Mother on you."

The little fellow tugged sharply on Spot's ear and sent him yelping away in hurt surprise.

Junior was very quiet for a long time as he sat in the tree. Finally he climbed down and found his sister.

"I'm sorry I pulled your hair yesterday," he said. "I'll let you play marbles with me right now, if you want."

Object Lesson Application

At the point where Daddy says, "I don't want to do anything that might hurt someone else," present the following object lesson as a verbal footnote to his statement: Display three large, white, paper hearts that have been taped together in a row side by side. One heart represents a person's own heart, and the others represent those of other people. The hearts are joined together to represent the influence, for bad or good, that people have on each other. If we do something wrong and blacken our lives with the black unhappiness of sin, we pull other people along with us. Bring the heart representing one's own heart into contact with a piece of black chalk or a burnt stick, blackening it. Cause the other hearts to follow in contacting the black surface. Show your congregation that all three hearts have been blackened. Turn them over to show sad expressions which have been painted on the back sides as part of your advance preparation. Sin always causes sadness. There is a sample sad expression depicted on page 94.

One could hold the black substance with a piece of paper, or wear a glove to keep from blackening his hand, or the black material (which could be a piece of paper) could be non-smearing with the backs of the hearts blackened in advance to make it appear like they had been blackened by the black material.

Picture or Chalk Application

When Daddy says, "I don't want to do anything that might hurt someone else," have him add, "Wrong things that I do always make bad impressions on other people's hearts." At this point draw the large heart shown in the illustration, using the flat side of a piece of red chalk. Now draw the hair pulling scene inside the heart in black outline. and tell how Junior suddenly discovered that his wrongdoing made an impression on the heart of the little boy next door.

Puppet Talk Application

Use a hand puppet to represent the little boy next door. Display a paper heart which represents Junior. Turn the heart over to show the words, "Hair pulling" on the back side, showing how Junior hurt his sister. Use the hand puppet to represent the little boy next door at play. Use your free hand to represent his dog running about him. Wiggle the four fingers which are held pointing down, to represent the dogs legs. Move this "running dog" back and forth in front of the puppet, and then have it pull the "dog's" tail, by having it pull the thumb of the hand representing the dog. Make the "dog" then run off. Next take a heart out from under the skirt of the puppet's costume to show that you are examining the heart of the little boy next door. On his heart you also discover the words, "Hair pulling," showing that Junior's action has influenced his neighbor's heart.

30

As for what was sown among thorns, this is he who hears the word, but the cares of the world and the delight in riches choke the word, and it proves unfruitful.—Matthew 13:22

Faith

10. The Too Busy Weed

Today I am going to tell you about a battle. This battle took place in a little girl's heart. Myopia had a faith in Jesus. Her faith made her love her Savior and attend church school, and be kind and good. This faith was like a flower that lived in her heart. There was also a weed that lived in her heart. It was a prickly nettle. The name of this weed was Too Busy. The Too Busy Weed was trying to shove Myopia's faith right out of her heart. This weed made her too busy to say her prayers at night, too busy to go to church school. She was too busy watching television, doing her homework, playing outdoors, and making clothes for her Garby doll. The busier Myopia became, the less time she had for Jesus. Her Too Busy Weed became bigger and bigger and it shoved harder and harder and took up more and more room, so that her faith slowly became crowded out of her heart. Finally the Too Busy Weed became so big that it had Myopia's faith crowded almost entirely out of her heart. It was just holding a grip on her heart with its finger tips.

"Help! help! help!" cried Myopia's faith to Myopia. "I'm being choked to death. Please don't be too busy to keep your faith alive."

What a tragedy was happening. Myopia was about to lose her faith. If she did she would never again be close to Jesus. She would never be able to work for him — to help in the work of his church — to live a fine joyous life in him. Her life would be wasted.

Just as Myopia's faith was almost dead she happened to read the words of Jesus in the thirteenth chapter of Matthew where he told how the seed of faith was sown on soil where weeds came up and choked it to death. Suddenly she realized that this was happening to her. She realized that many, many other children lost their faith in the same way, by just being too busy doing everyday things.

Just in the nick of time Myopia began to save her faith. Whenever it was time to say her prayers or go to church school, or do anything else for Jesus, she always did these things first and other things such as watching television were done later if there was time. She had learned how easy it was for everyday things to crowd faith right out of a person's heart.

Object Lesson Application

Show a large white paper heart. This is Myopia's heart. On the heart, near an edge, there is a flower which represents her faith. The flower is drawn in or cut out of a seed catalogue or cut from some other source. A strip of green paper has been cut along its top edge to appear like a row of grass stalks. Move this green strip, representing a row of weeds,

slowly across the face of the heart, starting at the opposite edge of the heart from where the flower is. Slowly the weeds will come to and cover the flower, thereby killing it.

As an optional embellishment, the back side of the heart could be black to show the emptiness that occurred when faith died.

When Myopia's faith is recovered, this can be shown by removing the "weeds" to show the flower again.

Picture or Chalk Talk Application

Draw the girl as shown. Next draw her heart and the flower of faith inside it, developing your presentation as indicated in object lesson application above. Next start drawing the weeds in the heart, using green chalk. Gradually cause them to obliterate the heart. Next draw in the tomb stone sticking out of the weeds to show that faith has almost died. Next tell how Myopia recovered her faith, without using chalk embellishments to depict this.

If you wish, you may first draw Myopia's mouth as just a small straight line, and after her faith has almost died enlarge this mouth to the expression of grief depicted.

Puppet Talk Application

Use a hand puppet to represent Myopia. It may be a two-faced or light bulb puppet with the change in expression occurring at the appropriate times. Prepare a paper heart that has a flower on one side of it and a row of weeds on the other. At the appropriate times remove this heart from under the puppet's skirt and show the flower in her heart, showing that she has faith; replace the heart; and again remove it and show the reverse side with the weeds, showing that faith has almost been choked out. See the object lesson application for the development of this application.

Jesus increased in wisdom and in stature,
and in favor with God and man.
—Luke 2:52

11.   The Boy with
the Baby Faith

Stagnation was the name of a boy who was almost grown. He was a very big boy, but he acted like a baby. He yelled so loudly at every meal that he blew the dishes off the table. He scolded his baby sister and made her cry. He refused to obey his mother. Finally she grabbed him by the feet and dragged him off to a doctor, to see what was the matter with him.

The doctor said, "The trouble with Stagnation is that he has the body of a big boy, but his faith in God never grew. He has the faith of a baby. No wonder he does such awful things. His baby faith inside his big body is like a pebble rattling around in a basket ball."

"How can I make my faith in God grow?" asked Stagnation.

"There is only one way to make faith grow," replied the doctor. You must add new Christian habits to your life. The reason you have only a baby faith is because you learned a little prayer and started going to church school when you were four years old and you have not added a single new Christian habit to your life since; so naturally your faith is only the size of a four-year-old baby's."

Stagnation yelled, "I do religious things. I read my Bible last year, once."

"That's just it," interrupted the doctor. "You read it *once* last year. If you are to grow in faith, the things you do for God must be a part of you. They must be done every day."

Stagnation began to add some Christian habits to his life. With each new habit, his faith grew. He began to pray every day, to read his Bible every day, to attend church and sing in the choir.

After a while he got tired and gave up some of these habits and immediately his faith shrank just that much. Finally he realized that his faith could only grow the size of his habits, so he kept adding new ones until he had a great big man-sized faith in God.

Object Lesson Application

Make a cardboard boy like the one in the picture talk illustration. His body is pleated, as indicated by the dotted lines in the illustration. The heavy line at the top of the row of words and the continuous line at the bottom also represent folds for this application. Show the cardboard boy, which represents Stagnation, with his folds folded. As he adds a new habit in the story, unfold that fold to reveal the appropriate word. As he discards habits, fold that word back up again. The boy's height will be shown to either grow or diminish.

Construction paper could be used for the boy. Also he could be made of filing cards taped together. If the cardboard is fairly stiff it could be cut in strips which would be joined together with tape, instead of folding the cardboard into layers.

Picture or Chalk Talk Application

Draw the head and arms as shown, down to the heavy black line. The folding body and legs have been made in advance, and are now stuck to the drawing with masking tape. The tape has been made into sticky-side-out circlets which have been placed in advance along the back, top of the body and leg piece. Develop your story as indicated in the object lesson application.

Puppet Talk Application

Use a hand puppet. The hand puppet will be used for Stagnation's head and arms. A folding body like that used in the object lesson application has been pinned with safety pins to the puppet costume just under the arms, to make an appearance similar to that of the picture talk application. Lesson development is the same as that for the object lesson application.

12. Hera's Glasses

Hera was a girl who found fault with everybody in school. When they had a popularity contest she got only two votes in spite of the fact that she voted for herself twice. She was hurt to have received so few votes. She started to cry.

She ran to the front of the class and yelled, "I don't care if this dirty old class doesn't like me. I hate every one of you. You are all so ugly you make me sick."

She was so angry that she held her breath until her face turned green. When she got home her mother looked at her and cried, "Hera has a green face!"

"Don't be silly," snorted her father, "Little girls just don't have greeeee, yiiii! She does have a green face."

Hera's face was such a bright green that it shone in the dark and kept her awake. She began to get sick from loss of sleep. Down she went from eighty pounds to seventy, to sixty, to forty, to twenty, to five. Finally she weighed only two and a half ounces and her parents thought she was sick enough to need to see a doctor.

At the doctor's office, Hera screamed, "Look at that horrid, wrinkled, old witch of a nurse!"

When she saw the doctor she screamed, "Look at that ugly doctor with a face like a mud turtle!"

The doctor examined Hera and murmured, "What this child needs is a new pair of glasses. Her eyes are so bad that all she can do is find fault with people. Here is a pair of glasses that will help her to see good things in people."

Hera put on the glasses. The doctor seemed to have such a

jolly, friendly face that she climbed up in his lap while he talked to her mother.

She smiled at the nurse on her way out. With her new glasses on, Hera thought the nurse had a gentle, kindly face, framed by beautiful white hair.

From that day on Hera was always able to see good in other people. She always expected them to do well in everything they tried. As a matter of fact, whenever the doctor had a patient who was discouraged with himself, he would send the patient to see Hera, and she would always find something wonderful about the patient, and cheer him up. Whenever Hera entered a room it always seemed like a ray of sunshine came in with her. Everybody loved Hera because one of the things this world needs is people who can see good in other people.

Object Lesson Application

In relating the story of Hera, put on a pair of dark glasses, to show that she saw people from a black point of view, and found fault. At the appropriate point, add red paper hearts over the dark lenses, to show that she now saw people with love. The hearts have been prepared for sticking by having sticky-side-out circlets of scotch tape on their backs.

Picture or Chalk Talk Application

Draw the girl as illustrated. The rectangular box to one side of her is not part of the chalk drawing, but is rather a paper cutout made in advance. The cutout has red heart shaped glasses drawn at the top of it and it is folded at the middle along the dotted line so that a smiling face painted on the bottom is out of sight. At the appropriate time in the story, show the cutout (with the smile folded out of sight), which represents Hera's new glasses. Place the glasses on the drawing of Hera and unfold the smile so that the cutout covers Hera's face and shows her with new glasses and a smile. Tape the cutout in place.

Puppet Talk Application

Tape a pair of red hearts over the puppet's eyes at the appropriate time in the story. The hearts should be large in relation to the size of the puppet's head, to aid audience visibility. Use sticky-side-out circlets of scotch tape on the backs of the hearts, or paper clips, to hold them in place. If you use tape, rub your fingers over the tape to diminish its stickiness, and place over the puppet's face lightly so as not to injure the surface of the puppet. Don't use tape on a paper puppet.

Use of a light puppet that changes its expression from a smile to a frown with the application of light, is optional. (See pages 94-95.)

Be Friendly

13.   The Sour Lemons

Nobody in the Lemon family ever smiled. They all looked like this: (Pull down the corners of your mouth with your fingers.) There were three children in the family. Their names were Gloomy, Glum, and Snobby.

There was no Sunday church school in the tiny town where they lived, so Father Lemon started one in his home. They sent out invitations to all the children in town, and waited hopefully on Sunday morning for them to come. When the town children arrived, Gloomy, Glum, and Snobby would not even say "hello" to them. Gloomy was too shy to do so. Glum was too busy talking to Snobby to do so, and Snobby thought he was to good to speak. So none of the children came back and they had to close their church school.

The Lemon family began attending church in a nieghboring town, but they were so unfriendly that they discouraged other people from attending there. Incidentally, I hope we don't have any unfriendly Lemons in our church.

Father Lemon started an ice cream business, but he frowned at his customers so hard it made their knees knock and they never came back again and his business failed.

Nobody liked the Lemons so the whole family just stayed home. They did nothing all day long but drink vinegar and sit around in a circle and frown at each other. They frowned so much it made their mouths and eyebrows ache.

Finally Glum got so tired of sitting down and frowning that he stood on his head and frowned. An upside frown is a smile, so it looked like he was smiling. Father Lemon was so surprised to see what looked like a smile that he started to laugh. Mother Lemon began to giggle. They all roared with laughter. Their faces felt so much better that they never frowned again.

Object Lesson Application

Use a lemon with a painted expression of gloom on it, or a yellow construction paper cutout copy of our illustration. At the appropriate time you could show the reverse side of your lemon, which has a smile (similar to that shown on page 69) on it.

Picture or Chalk Talk Application

Drawn as illustrated.

Puppet Talk Application

Use a yellow light bulb hand puppet. (Pages 93-96.) Turn the yellow light on at those times when you specifically mention the Lemon's unhappiness. Change expressions at the appropriate times.

14. Jack Sprat

Jack Sprat could eat no fat,
His wife could eat no lean;
And so betwixt them both,
They licked the platter clean.

Little Sam yelled, "I hate sisters. You always want your own way. I'm going to put on our puppet show about Jack Sprat all by myself, without you."

Sam's sister, Sandra, screamed, "Well, I hate brothers. I can put on a better show without you. Your ideas aren't any good."

Sam got busily to work trying to sew a costume for his Jack Sprat puppet.

"Ouch!" he roared, "That's the millionth time I've struck my finger with this needle. Phooey, I'm not going to give a puppet show."

"Boys can't sew," sneered Sandra as she tried to hammer some boards together to make her puppet stage. Suddenly she threw the hammer across the room and began to cry while Sam laughed.

"That hurts to hit your thumb with a hammer," sobbed Sandra.

Suddenly uproarious laughter filled the room. The puppets were laughing at the children.

The Jack Sprat puppet said, "You silly children. You are missing the whole point of the nursery rhyme. Jack Sprat and his wife were different, he couldn't eat fat meat and she couldn't eat lean meat; but instead of fighting they worked together and they got along fine."

Sandra laughed, "Girls can sew and boys can hammer and saw, so we can work together and make our show."

42

"Yeah," replied her brother, "It's a good thing we aren't both boys or both girls. I guess that's the reason God made people different, so they could work together."

Object Lesson Application

Make large paper cutouts of a hammer and a needle. They have smiles on one side and frowns on the back side. (See page 69 for suggested expressions) Their expressions are changed at the proper times in the story.

Picture or Chalk Talk Application

Draw as illustrated.

Puppet Talk Application

Boy and girl hand puppets (see pages 96-97) first fight each other and then put their arms around each other.

You are all one in Christ Jesus.
—Galatians 3:28

15. The Leopard Skin

Mrs. Next Door Neighbor asked Mother why little Tim played with a small boy of another race, with a different colored skin.

Mother answered, "I don't think Tim even notices what color his friend's skin is. All Tim knows is that he has a wonderful friend, and that such minor differences do not matter at all. If Tim paid attention to such a little thing as skin color, it would rob him of a wonderful friendship. Let me tell you a true story:

"When some faithful missionaries in Africa were preparing to leave on furlough, the natives held a farewell service and presented them with a beautiful leopard skin. An elderly woman who had never spent a day in school, made a presentation speech, which showed knowledge that comes from God.

She said, "This is our greeting to the church in America. We think this is a very beautiful skin. It is not all white, nor all black. It is both white and black. That is why it is beautiful. That is the way with God's great human family. We are not all white and we are not all black. We are both black and white. And if the black folks and the white folks will help each other and live together in harmony, then God's great human family will be beautiful."

Object Lesson Application

Show a cutout of a leopard, made from a printed picture, or made by copying our illustration.

Picture or Chalk Talk Application

Draw as illustrated. The dots are made with flat lengthwise strokes of the chalk, and while not technically correct, will serve the purpose.

Use a leopard glove puppet. (See pages 96-97.)

If any one strikes you on the right cheek,
turn to him the other also.

—Matthew 5:39

16. The Cat Chaser

Mother opened the kitchen window and yelled at little Ann, "Where are you going with that pitchfork?"

"I'm going to kill the White's dog so it won't chase my poor little kitties," replied Ann.

"Come inside," Mother commanded. "Don't you remember what you heard in church school about Jesus telling us to turn the other cheek?"

"Yeah, but Mom," wailed Ann, "That doesn't help my poor little innocent kittens."

"Let's sit down and think and pray about it," replied Mother. "I think we can think of a way that will not make the neighbors angry with us. We have wonderful neighbors and it is much more important to have friends for neighbors, than to worry about a little cat chasing. Let me tell you a true story about a sheepman in Indiana.[1] Dogs were killing his sheep and ruining his business. He could have made enemies by hitting back with a lawsuit, or a barbed wire fence, or even killing the dogs with a shotgun, which are ways that sheepmen usually take. Instead he thought of a wonderful way to do something kind for his neighbors, but if you are sure that turning the other cheek doesn't work you won't want to hear what he did."

"Aw come on, tell me, Mom."

Mother smiled, "He gave all the neighbor children a lamb or two as pets. Soon his neighbors had little flocks of their own and they

1 Adapted from an account given by J. Wallace Hamilton in *The Thunder of Bare Feet*, Fleming H. Revell Co.

began to keep their dogs tied up. Ann! How can I talk to you when you run out of the house like that?"

In a little while Ann came back into the house saying, "Know where I've been Mom? I just gave the Smiths one of my little kitties, and besides their dog never catches my kitties. He just likes to chase them."

Object Lesson Application

Use a toy dog or a cutout of a dog, copying our illustration, or cutting out a picture from another source. Show the dog as being leashed to two different retainers. This is done by having two strings tied around the dog's neck. One is tied to a paper heart, and the other is tied to a paper shotgun representing hate. Hold up the two retainers, to the audience's view, alternately. State that love is a better way of keeping a dog from killing sheep, than hate.

Picture or Chalk Talk Application

Draw the dog as illustrated, without his wagging tail or the heart. State that love makes the best leash to keep a dog from killing sheep. Add the heart and the wagging tail. Change the dog's expression as shown by the arrow that points to the smiling expression above the dog's head. This smiling head is not a separate drawing, but shows the way in which the dog's face is now modified. Extend the snarling mouth with lines going upward, to make it into a smile. Enlarge the dog's eye so it covers the front part of the frowning eyebrow, which will extend out of the eye as the top line of three smile wrinkles.

Puppet Talk Application

Use a dog glove puppet. (See pages 96-97.) Have a string attached to a paper heart around the dog's neck. Explain as described above.

Rejoice always. . . . Give thanks in all circumstances; for this is the will of God.
—I Thessalonians 5:16, 18

Thankful

17. Rubbers That Ruined a Day

It had rained the night before. Mud and puddles were everywhere. Mother insisted that Chris wear rubbers to school. You would think she had asked him to wear a dress, the way he fussed. He cried and stormed. He refused to go to school. He told his mother that none of the other boys would wear rubbers and they would all call him a sissy. He finally got to school, and he was angry all day long. He refused to answer when his teacher spoke to him, and he had to stay after school.

Chris was always getting very upset about small things. That night he refused to eat his entire supper because his mother had served asparagus, which he did not like.

Chris's father, who was a doctor, decided to do something about his son.

"Come on Chris," he said. "You are going to the children's hospital with me."

"What for, Daddy? I'm not sick."

Father insisted, "You're going anyway."

At the hospital they talked to a small boy without any legs and a girl who was blind. They saw many children with very serious diseases and handicaps.

On the way home, Chris said, "I know why you took me to the hospital now, Dad. I will never again let little things like rubbers or asparagus keep me from being happy about all the good things I have."

Father looked pleased, "Son, our Heavenly Father has given us so many wonderful gifts, that it is our duty to praise him every day and be thinkful."

49

Object Lesson Application

Use any object to represent a minor irritation. Possible objects would be a pair of rubbers (which bothered Chris), or a bandage on a finger, or a flyswatter. In the latter cases, alternate the story to make Chris' day ruined by a cut finger, or a troublesome fly.

Picture or Chalk Talk Application

Draw as illustrated. Change this story to make Chris' day ruined by a troublesome mosquito which bites him. The mosquito, although very small, is shown as very large, because Chris lets this small thing take on large proportions.

Puppet Talk Application

Develop as indicated above in the picture talk application. Use a mosquito glove puppet (see pages 96-97) which plagues and threatens a much smaller cardboard cutout of a boy.

An alternate application, based on the object lesson application, would be to show a hand puppet, cast as Chris, that has a bandaged finger, or that has a flyswatter taped to its hand.

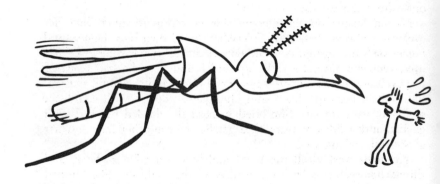

18.   The Black and Blue Glasses

Moana was a little girl who wore glasses that were so dirty that she could only see the colors, black and blue. She spent all of her time drawing pictures because she wanted to be an artist when she grew up. Of course she only used the colors, black and blue. When she drew pictures of the outdoors, they were always filled with big black rain clouds. When she drew pictures of her garden, she did not draw all the beautiful red, yellow, blue, and violet flowers, she only drew the weeds.

Moana looked on the gloomy side of things so much that her eyebrows always frowned. Everyday her frown got bigger and bigger and her eyebrows went down further and further over her eyes. One morning she woke up and found that she had frowned her eyebrows down all the way over her eyes and she could not see. She put on her dirty black and blue glasses, but she still could not see. She began to cry. She cried so hard she flooded her bed with gallons and gallons of tears. She got her hair and her face and her glasses all soaking wet.

The tears washed all the black and blue dirt off her glasses and shrank her eyebrows back up in place so she could see. She blinked her eyes. With her clean glasses she saw all the other colors, red, orange, yellow, green, blue, purple, and white. She leaped for joy at such beauty. She ran and grabbed her color crayons and took all her rain pictures and drew in beautiful rainbows. She took all her weed pictures and drew in beautiful flowers. Moana had learned that the difference between being happy and sad lay in whether or not you look at the gloomy or bright side of things.

51

Object Lesson Application

Make a black cloud out of construction paper. Cut out a bow shaped piece of white paper and color it to resemble a rainbow. In telling the story, show the black cloud with the rainbow concealed behind it. At the proper time bring the rainbow into view.

Picture or Chalk Talk Application

Draw the smiling face in advance. The hair shown to the right of the girl is not a part of the chalk picture, but is a cutout made of yellow paper, with a red bow. The cutout is a paper wig which can be shown from both sides. It has a sticky-side-out circlet of masking tape on either side of it. The paper wig is used to change the girl's expression by alternately covering each of her two faces. When you appear before your congregation, the wig is seen, in place on the drawing board, and

is hiding the smiling face. Another bit of advance preparation would be to have light pencil marks marking the facial boundaries that you must keep inside of in drawing. In front of your congregation, draw the frowning face and the rest of the girl. Draw the rain cloud, shading it with a few strokes made with the flat of the chalk. The rainbow is drawn next with strokes made with the flat sides of red, orange, green, blue, and purple chalk. (Yellow chalk won't show up well on newsprint). At the proper time, replace the wig over the frowning face to show Moana smiling.

Puppet Talk Application

Use a hand puppet with the application and objects specified in the object lesson application. The puppet is Moana, who is shown to be either looking at the gloomy side or the bright side of life. Glasses on the puppet should not be used, as they are not necessary.

Use of a two-faced or expression-changing light bulb hand puppet are optional. (See pages 94-95.)

Her children rise up and call her blessed.
—Proverbs 31:28

19. Mommies

Daddy and the neighbors were driving around in their cars, looking all over for little Margaret. They found her only a block or two from home sitting on a doorstep crying.

"Why did you run away from home, Margaret?" asked Daddy.

"I don't like Mommy," pouted Margaret. "She's too bossy. She makes me clean up my room. She makes me make my bed and wash the dishes. She makes me go to bed when I want to watch television."

A week later Mother had to go to the hospital for an operation. How little Margaret missed her mother then. There was no one to hold her when she fell down and hurt her knee. No one who could cook as well as Mother. No one to read her Bible stories at night. All day long Margaret missed her mother.

The next day when Daddy was about to visit Mother at the hospital Margaret asked him to help her write a letter to Mommy. Daddy got out a pencil and paper and wrote down what Margaret said.

Here is what Daddy wrote: "Dear Mommy I love you. I never knew how many things you do for me all of the time until you were sick at the hospital. You do a million things for me every day. Please hurry and get well and I will do what you ask me right away. Love, Margaret."

Daddy took Margaret in his arms and said, "We miss Mommy when she's not here, don't we Margaret? Mommies are one of the nicest things God ever made."

Object Lesson Application

Display a "treasure chest" made out of any box, such as a match box. The only preparation needed will be to cover the printed sides of the box that might face the congregation, with paper. It is not necessary to paint on details to make the box look authentic. In telling the story, cause Margaret to wish to leave home, not only because of dissatisfaction, but also to find a pirates treasure chest, so she can have everything she wants. (Display your treasure chest.) At the end of the story Margaret discovers that a mommy is the most wonderful treasure any child can have. Open the treasure chest and remove a "mommy." This can either be a small adult type doll, or a cutout of a lady taken from a mail order catalog.

Picture or Chalk Talk Application

Draw the treasure chest as illustrated. The drawing paper has been prepared in advance with a slit along the line that is to be drawn to form the top of the chest (under the lid). In back of the slit there is an envelope which holds a cardboard cutout of a mother, similar to the one shown in the illustration. The lady in the illustration represents this cutout, which is to be removed from the chest at the proper time and, of course, is not drawn to the side of the chest. Develop this application in the manner suggested for the object talk application.

Puppet Talk Application

Develop as suggested in the object talk application, with a hand puppet cast in the role of Margaret. The sermonizer relates the fact that Margaret ran away from home and asks her why. She whispers her answer in his ear, which he repeats out loud as she supposedly says it. The sermonizer displays a treasure chest like the one Margaret is seeking. Then the sermonizer relates the rest of the story and removes the paper mother from the chest.

Be of good cheer, I have overcome the
world.—John 16:33

Resurrection

20.   The Bird
on the Cross[1]

On Easter Sunday the people came to church, but their faces
were the same as usual. The people who were usually smiling were
smiling as usual, and the usual frowners were frowning as usual,
and those who usually had blank faces were wearing them just as
blank as ever.

The little bird who lived in the church belfry could not understand this, Everybody should be shouting for joy on Easter, thought
the bird. Didn't the people know that Christ their Savior had risen
from the dead? The tomb was empty and Christ was watching over
them and loving them this very minute?

The little bird flew in a window and looked at the solemn
people. Perhaps these people don't know that Jesus is risen from
the dead, thought the bird. "I must remind them that the cross is
empty and Christ is risen. I will perch on top of that wooden cross
in front of the church, and sing with all my heart so that the people
will notice that the cross is empty and Jesus is risen."

The heads of all of the people turned to watch as the little bird
flew just over their new Easter hats and landed on the cross in front.
There he threw back his head, puffed out his little chest, and began to sing for all he was worth. Everyone began to smile when he
heard the little bird's happy song. The church organist stopped
playing so everyone could hear it better.

The minister spoke, "Thank you, little bird, for reminding us
that the cross is empty and that we should all be praising God
today."

1 The idea for this story was taken from an article by Nevin Feather in the March-
April, 1963 issue of *The Upper Room.*

Object Lesson Application

Display a cutout of a bird. Cause the bird to fly and perch on a cardboard cross.

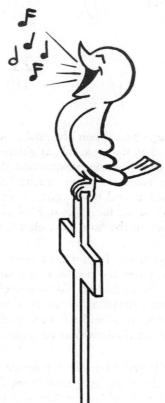

Picture or Chalk Talk Application

Draw as illustrated.

Puppet Talk Application

Use a bird glove puppet. (See pages 96-97.) Cause the bird to fly to and perch on a cardboard or three dimensional cross.

I can do all things in him who strengthens me. —Philippians 4:13

21.   Olga's Big Eyes

Little Olga had big eyes. When she had a job to do her eyes made the job look so big, that it would frighten her half to death. If she had a sweater to knit, in her imagination she would see every stitch that had to be taken. So many stitches! She would get exhausted thinking about it and never start. If she had to mow the lawn she would think of all the thousands of blades of grass that had to be cut, and fall to the floor exhausted from thinking about it.

One day she came home from school with twenty arithmetic problems to do. She spent ten minutes just sitting in her chair worrying about how she could ever do so many problems. Finally she watched a television program. By the time it was over she had just as much homework to do and less time to do it in. This worried her so much she watched another program, and another until it was time for bed.

During the night she had a horrible nightmare. She dreamed that a giant arithmetic book, as big as a house, was chasing her. It was just about to snap shut its covers on her and eat her the way a chicken would peck up a worm when she screamed. She screamed so loud she blew the roof off her house. Of course, her father called the fire department and the firemen put the roof back on. Olga had the same dream over again and screamed again and the poor firemen had to come a second time. However, Olga had the dream over again a third time and this time the firemen seemed impatient so Olga's father also called a doctor. The doctor gave Olga some eye-shrinking medicine so she only could see a little bit of her

59

work at a time — so that if she had to knit a sweater, she could only see the first stitch that had to be taken, or if she had to do arithmetic problems, she could only see one of them at a time.

The next day Olga again had twenty arithmetic problems to do, but with her shrunken eyes, she could only see one problem on the entire page that had to be done.

"Ha, only one problem," thought Olga. "I can do that easily."

Olga ran home, leaped into her study chair, and went right to work and did the only problem she could see in no time at all. When this problem was over her shrunken eyes saw one more problem that needed to be done, which did not look like much so she did this. This continued until all of her homework was done.

Now Olga loves to get her work done, for she has learned that she only has do a thing one step at a time, and anybody can do that.

Object Lesson Application

Display a paper doll, doll, or hand puppet (without your hand in it) trapped under a load of school books. Tape a pair of glasses on the doll at the proper time in the story and show that she has mastered the problem of work by having her sit on top of the books.

Picture or Chalk Talk Application

Develop as indicated above. First draw the books and then draw Olga trapped beneath them. At the end draw her sitting on top of them. It will not be necessary to get rid of the Olga beneath the books. One picture is her "before," and the other is her "after." In drawing the top book, do not complete the lines that would be in the way when Olga is drawn on top.

Puppet Talk Application

Use a two faced or light bulb puppet, that changes its expression into a smile when the light is turned on. (See pages 94-95.) Present in the manner indicated in the object lesson application, with the puppet smiling at the proper time, and with the books used.

All Scripture is inspired by God and profitable ... for training in righteousness.
—II Timothy 3:16

22.   A Book to Grow By

Alan was sitting in Grandpa's lap listening to Bible stories.

"No matter what happened," exclaimed Alan, "Jesus always knew what to do. Didn't he Gramp?"

"That's right," replied Grandpa. "Jesus knew what to do when he saw sick, and lame, and blind people. He knew what to do when people wanted to learn new and wonderful things about God. He knew what to do in terrible storms when gigantic waves threatened to turn his boat over. He knew what to do when a mob of angry men with swords came to kill him. He always did the right thing."

"How did Jesus know what to do, Gramp?"

"Well," answered Grandpa, "one way he knew was by talking to God very often in prayer."

"I know another way," interrupted Alan. "He knew his Bible real well. You told me yesterday about how Jesus' family paid a visit to Jerusalem and left for three whole days and they couldn't find Jesus because he had stayed behind asking the teachers in the church there questions. Wow! Jesus talked to those teachers all day long for days. He sure must have wanted to know about the Bible."

"Gramp," continued Alan, "do you think I could grow to be a real good man and live a life that would help other people if I pray every day and read my Bible?"

"I'm sure of it," replied Grandpa. "There have been lots of great Christian men and women who have done wonderful things for God, and they all have spent much time in prayer and known their Bible well."

Object Lesson Application

Display a Bible. Before telling the story, comment that some people read their Bibles very little. For them it is just a book full of old memories, like faded flowers that are pressed in a book. These people will not grow from their Bible reading. Their faith is apt to be sort of pressed and dead like this flower. (Remove either a pressed flower from the Bible, or a paper imitation of one, such as the one in our illustration.) Other people study their Bibles everyday and it helps them to gain a strong, happy faith. (Remove a large heart to demonstrate. This heart may have a smiling face such as shown, and it may have some device attached to it to show strength, such as a pair of muscular arms or a picture of a dynamo or an electric motor.

Other things which might be removed from the Bible, in this or another object talk, are a pocket mirror, a road map, and a cardboard cutout of a bottle of milk, to show that in the Bible we find a mirror of, and a better understanding of our secret faults, guidance in life, and food for spiritual growth.

Picture or Chalk Talk Application

Draw as illustrated, using the method described above.

Puppet Talk Application

Use the presentation and the objects described in the object lesson application, but add a hand puppet cast in the role of Alan. The sermonizer could cast himself in the role of Grandpa and give all of his dialogue in answer to Alan's questions. (See page 98 for ways to make a puppet "talk.")

He who loves his life loses it, and he who
hates his life in this world will keep it for
eternal life.—John 12:25

love 23.　　　The Lost
Load

Laddy had been naughty at summer camp. He got away from
his counselor and fell over a bank, broke his arm and got his body
covered with hives from poison ivy. His face was so swollen that
none of his friends recognized him. He itched so much he could
hardly stand it. However, his counselor was very patient. He drove
Laddy to the doctor's office to get his arm set and waited on him
constantly.

"I don't see why you waste so much time helping me," said
Laddy to his counselor.

The counselor replied, "I like helping you. We are not really
happy ourselves unless we help others; because God made us that
way. When you see someone who is gloomy and feeling sorry for
himself, you know he is thinking about himself. When we help
with someone else's burden, our own load goes away."

Later that day, Laddy sat on the bank of the river and watched
the other children swim. He loved to swim more than anything else
but, of course, he could not go in. His arm ached like a sore tooth.
He itched all over. He listened to the happy shouts of his friends.
He had come to camp to have a good time and now it was all
ruined. He remembered how his counselor had said, "When we
help with someone else's burden, our own load goes away."

"Baloney," thought Laddy, "nothing could make me feel good
right now."

Just then Laddy saw Winfield, the little boy who was visiting
camp that afternoon with his father. He was hardly more than a
toddler. Winfield stumbled over a tree root and the box of popcorn

that he had been eating so contentedly spilled all over the ground. Winfield felt about the ground, trying to find his popcorn. Suddenly Laddy realized that Winfield was completely blind.

"Come on," said Laddy, "I'll help you pick up that dirty popcorn and go buy you another box. I have some money in the camp bank."

Laddy took Winfield's hand and led him back to the camp store. He took him all over the camp and explained everything to him. He let him feel the tents and the cots. Laddy had only known Winfield for a couple of hours, but already he felt that he loved the little fellow. In spite of his blindness, he was such a cheerful boy. Winfield laughed at Laddy's jokes, and seemed to appreciate everything Laddy did for him.

When Winfield's father came to take him home, Winfield said, "Daddy, this is my friend, Laddy. He 'splained the whole camp to me. He's the nicest boy in the whole world. When I get home you are going to help me write a letter for him."

Winfield insisted on kissing Laddy goodbye.

Laddy felt ten feet tall. As a matter of fact, just then he did not have a care in the world.

Object Lesson Application

Display a rough-shaped, black, paper oval, which is described as a load. Remark that everyone has some load to bear. Tell about Laddy and his load. Tell how Laddy showed love to Winfield. Fasten a red paper heart over the black paper "load," securing it with a sticky-side-out circlet of masking tape which has been fixed to the back of the heart. The heart represents love and assistance. When the heart is in place and at the proper time in the story, unfold paper wings, which are folded in back of the heart. This represents the fact that when we help someone else, our own load takes wings and flies away. If you make the wings smaller in proportion to the heart shown in the drawing, and make the wings and heart similar to the drawing, the wings will easily fold out of sight behind the heart.

Picture or Chalk Talk Application

Develop this application in the same manner as the object lesson application above. First draw the boy and his heavy load. At the proper time add what is shown here as a dotted line, but which will be drawn as a continuous line. This turns the load into a load with a heart on top of it. At the proper time add the wings and the shadow underneath the boy and change the boy's expression into a smile like that shown on the face to the left of the boy. This is done by extending and enlarging the sorrowful mouth into a smile. The head to the left of the boy is not meant to be drawn beside the boy, but merely shows an alteration to be made in the boy's face.

Puppet Talk Application

Develop this application in the same manner as that indicated for the object lesson application. Use a hand puppet. Hold the puppet in a bent over position so that his back presents a horizontal surface. Place a "heavy" load upon his back. The load can be a wad of dark paper, or a sock stuffed with some other socks to have a ball-like appearance. Apply a paper heart of the kind described above to the load, sticking it there with tape. At the proper time, open the hidden wings and make the load "fly" off of the puppet's back.

24. The Girl Who Saw Good in Others

In a dark woods there was a terrible robber who lived with a horrible wife who nagged and yelled at him with a voice that sounded like a herd of angry elephants trumpeting. The robber's father, who was a drunken bum, lived with them. He did nothing all day but lie around in a drunken stupor and carve sticks of wood.

One night the robber woke up and discovered that someone had entered his house and was asleep on the living room rug. It was a little girl named Joy. She was sleeping with her head on her handbag.

The robber gently lifed her and put her on the sofa so he could steal her handbag. Just then Joy woke up.

"I knew you wouldn't mind if I came into your house to sleep," she smiled. "I was lost in the woods. You remind me of my daddy. You are handsome and kind like he is."

The robber almost fell over in surprise. Nobody had ever told him he was handsome and kind before. He ran to look in the mirror.

As they all sat down to breakfast, the horrible wife was getting ready to curse her husband, when Joy cried out, "What a wonderful cook you are. My! those pancakes smell good."

The horrible wife stood there with her mouth open. If this dear child thought she was wonderful, she should not yell at her husband just now.

After breakfast Joy looked at some of the animals that the drunken father had carved. Her eyes grew wide with admiration.

"You must be the best carver in the whole world," she said.

The old drunk had started to reach for his whiskey, but he

stopped. If the little girl thought he was wonderful, perhaps he should not disappoint her.

Little Joy had to wait several weeks for her father to come and get her, so she lived with the robber and his family. Before she left their lives were completely changed. She thought they were so wonderful, that they began to act like good people rather than disappoint her.

After Joy left the reformed robber, she had many happy adventures. Her heart was so full of love that she could always see good in people and wherever she went she always made people better.

Is this story true? Yes and no. It did not really happen exactly like this, but I do know some people who always see good in others, and they really do make other people better, and it really does seem as though God is very close when they are around.

Object Lesson Application

Display a paper doll, or a girl cutout made from a picture in a mail order catalog. The girl has large red hearts on her face to serve as eyes, showing that she sees through the eyes of love. This girl represents Joy. When the fact develops in the narration, that she brings out good in others, cause a cross to be seen shining through her body. (Body has cardboard cross glued to back. Shine light through it.)

Picture or Chalk Talk Application

Draw a picture of a heart and turn it into the robber, with a frown on his face. The heart shows that there is hidden good in him. Draw the picture of a little girl, to his side, next. Her heart-shaped eye shows that she sees good in him. As a result of this he changes from a frowning evil man to a smiling good man. The bottom, heart-faced man is not an additional picture to be drawn on paper, but is the second stage of the robber. It shows how more moustache is added to cover up his angry mouth, and how a smiling mouth is added beneath it. It also shows how the robber's eyebrows have their lines extended into a half circle, and how pupils are added in those half circles, so that his frowning eyebrows become the bottom lines of smiling eyes. Up-turned eyebrows are also added. The man has his face changed at the appropriate time in the story.

Puppet Talk Application

Use a puppet like the kinds described on page 93. Cause a cutout of girl, like that described in the object lesson application above, to be brought into the puppet's presence. The puppet represents the robber. When the cutout sees good in the robber, he changes and Christ is seen to be in his life. Show the cross shining in or through the robber's face (a light bulb puppet face).

I came that they may have life, and have
it abundantly.—John 10:10

Faith

25.   Medicine
or Food

There was a boy named Lagg, who thought that religion was like bad tasting medicine. Whenever he had to go to church school or say his prayers, he made a horrible face and stuck out his tongue just like I am doing now, and just the way a person would do if they had to take bitter medicine.

Lagg had a twin brother named Leap, who thought that religion was like good tasting food, such as chocolate milk. He loved to go to church and say his prayers, and do kind things.

When summer time came, Lagg took a vacation from going to church, as though it were a kind of bothersome work, but Leap went to church all summer long because he thought of it as a pleasure.

When they grew older Lagg noticed that Leap's faith in God meant a great deal to him. Leap's face glowed with happiness when he said his prayers or went to church. Lagg wished with all of his heart that he had a wonderful faith like that of Leap.

One day when the boys were at the doctor's office, Lagg asked the doctor to take an X-ray picture of their faith so he could see why Leap had so much more fun with his religion than did Lagg. Under the X-ray machine, Lagg's faith looked like a pathetic little, sick, dried-up dwarf. Lagg was ashamed of it. However, Leap's faith looked like a great, strong giant in shining armor.

"The reason for this is very clear," said the doctor. "Lagg has treated religion like medicine, and hated it. Therefore he has done as little as possible to make his faith grow. However, Leap has loved his faith and it has been food to his soul and it made it grow big and strong and wonderful."

When Lagg heard this he began to work at his faith with all of his heart and soon he began to think that serving and loving God was the nicest thing a person can do. As a matter of fact the next time he had his faith X-rayed it had already started to grow bigger and stronger.

Object Lesson Application

Display a medicine bottle and a bottle of milk.

Picture or Chalk Talk Application

Draw as illustrated. The knight may be shaded with flat strokes of blue chalk.

Puppet Talk Application

Use a hand puppet. Use safety pins to add material to its skirt, so that it extends down below your elbow when your hand is in it. Display a medicine bottle and a milk bottle. The same puppet represents the souls of both Lagg and Leap. A the proper times show Lagg clasping the medicine bottle. The dwarfed nature of his soul is shown by having the puppet skirt bunched up to make the puppet look as short as possible. At the proper time show the puppet as Leap clasping, and possibly pretending to drink from, the milk bottle. If the bottle is of glass, the fact that it is empty will not matter. If the milk container is of cardboard, this will be so much the better. Show the fine, big appearance of Leap's soul by pulling the puppet costume down to make the puppet look as tall as possible.

Love does not insist on its own way.
—I Corinthians 13:5

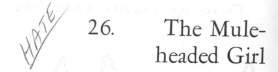

26. The Mule-headed Girl

There was a little girl who was called Mulie, because she was as stubborn as a mule. She always wanted her own way. For instance, when she played at the home of her friend, May, and May wanted to play rocket ship, Mulie would say, "No, if you don't play house, I'm going home and never speak to you again!"

If they played house and May wanted to be the mother, Mulie would insist on being the mother herself, and make May the child. If May wanted to play house on the porch, Mulie would insist on playing under the trees. They usually spent more time fighting than playing. They would argue over everything. Then they would get angry and hit each other and Mulie would go home and sulk.

No matter where Mulie was, she would insist on her own way, and she would kick and scream and cry if she did not get it. Pretty soon nobody wanted to have anything to do with her. Naturally Mulie was very unhappy for that is the way with selfish people.

To make matters worse, Mulie's head started to change into a mule's head. Short, grey hair started to grow all over her face and her ears started to get longer and longer. Sometimes when she cried and screamed for her own way her voice even sounded like a donkey braying, "hee haw, hee haw." All the newspaper reporters flocked in to take pictures and write stories about this strange girl.

One day Mulie learned that her friend May was moving away, so she went over to say goodbye and play with her one last time. She decided to be very nice to May as this would be the last time she would ever see her. She let May have her own way in everything. They played rocket ship and May was the captain.

Mulie and May had more fun playing together that way than ever before. It was much more fun when one did not insist on her own way all of the time. In fact Mulie had so much fun that she never insisted on her own way again, and people began to like her instead of avoiding her. They even changed her name to Julie.

The next time a crowd of reporters came to take a picture of the

girl with a mule's head, they discovered that her head had changed back into a little girl's head.

"I'm sorry," Julie told the reporters, "but there's no mule-headed girl living here now, and you'll never, never find her here again."

Object Lesson Application

Display a cut out picture of a mule or donkey's head. At the proper time in the story, turn the picture around to reveal a picture of a girl's head. This head has been pasted to the back of the mule's picture. The heads can be obtained from magazines or copied from our illustrations.

Picture or Chalk Talk Application

Draw the mule as illustrated. The picture to the right of the mule shows lines which are to made to modify its appearance. This is not a second picture to be drawn beside the mule. After the mule picture has been modified as illustrated, and at the appropriate time in the story, tear the picture off of the easel, turn the picture upside down (so that the mule is seen to have changed into the likeness of a girl), and show to the congregation. You will note that the features of the girl are drawn into the mule, while the girl is upside down.

The original story-sermon should be modified for the chalk talk presentation. Here May prefers to play cowboy instead of wanting to play house. When Mulie goes over to play with May for the last time, say that she donned her cowboy hat and put her long cowboy handkerchief around her neck before going over.

Puppet Talk Application

Use a mule glove puppet. (See pages 96-97.) If desired you can have the face of a girl taped, with a sticky-side-out circlet of masking tape, or pinned, to the back of the puppet's head, so that you can turn the back of its head to the congregation and show the girl's face.

CHILDREN'S
SERMON TECHNIQUES

STORY SERMONS

Criteria of Suitability

Children's sermons should be adapted to the understanding of a child. For instance, a sermon on humility might better deal with children who show off in front of their class, instead of telling how a general in the army was humble enough to help some private dig a ditch. A sermon on the nature of God might better compare his love to that of an earthly parent, than to deal with the nature of the Trinity. A small child does not have enough understanding of the nature of the members of the Trinity individually, to make even the simplest explanation of the Trinity of meaning to him.

Another example of a poor children's sermon is one where the teacher holds up a clear pane of glass and a mirror, declaring that the love of money is evil because the silvered mirror back, in contrast with the clear glass, prevents one from seeing other people through it, but rather limits one's gaze to himself. Whereas a child is old enough to share his allowance in the work of Christ, he is not old enough to be in a position where monetary considerations could dominate his life and shut out his sensitivity to others.

In preparing a children's sermon, one should ask himself whether or not he has ever seen, or heard of, a child actually doing the things about which he would speak. If, after a children's sermon, a parent is able to say to a child, "See, the minister was talking about you this morning," it is an indication that the talk was appropriate.

Although children's sermons should usually be about things that children actually do, this should not rule out the inclusion of stories about the lives of great people. A child is quite capable of having such stories mold his life. Whereas a child cannot immediately do such a thing as serve as a foreign missionary, he can think about such things. A child's goals and concepts of his future self are very much a part of his present life.

One should be careful not to talk down to a child. A child's understanding is far more advanced than his ability to express himself. A small child can draw a picture of a man that consists of stick-like arms and legs coming off a big, round, bodyless head. However the same child would immediately know that something was wrong if he saw a lifelike doll that had the body omitted. Children watch television and are observers of the adult world, and understand more of this world than many people realize.

One should avoid the story-sermon that uses a moral of vague relationship to the story. If a story is to be about a childish foible, let it be about that foible from start to finish. For example, one should avoid telling a story about how an aviator flew his plane high enough to make a rat in it die of oxygen starvation, and then urging children to similarly live on a high plane. Flying an airplane high is not the same as living on a high level. Furthermore, although one can avoid certain temptations through a highly moral life, and although heights do kill rats, it is not true that moral living avoids temptations *because* heights kill rats.

Methods of Gaining Interest

To add interest and better to strike home with a moral, a children's sermon should be specific in identifying faults or virtues. Do not merely say, "Sonny is a gossip," but say, "Sonny said, 'Joe has a big, fat mother.' " Do not say, "Sonny gave money to benevolences," but say, "Sonny gave his fifty cents to help a little boy in India learn to love Jesus." Do not say, "The children were always fighting," but say, "Sally ran to Mother yelling, 'Mommy, Sonny is spitting on me!' "

It will be helpful, in preparing children's sermons, to keep a record of the actual good and bad deeds of children that one knows.

A story will hold juvenile interest far better than a lecture that consists of only one moralizing sentence after another. If one is sensitive to audience empathy, it is possible to sense interest rapidly waning at the point where one completes a children's story-sermon and starts tacking a moral onto it.

Regardless of whether a children's sermon is an object sermon or not, it is advantageous for it to be centered around a mental picture of an object that is captivating to the imagination. It is easier for a child to remember stories about such themes as dirty pigs that gossip, or irreverent donkeys in church, or selfish octopuses, than it is for him to remember such abstract themes as "kindness in speech," or "reverence in church,' or "sharing one's possessions."

If an actual object or picture is shown with a sermon, retention is increased many fold. Three days after Sunday, many a child would be able to say, "I saw a pig in church that said bad things"; but how many would be able even to remember the theme of an abstract sermon on kindliness in speech?

Much of the success of a children's sermon depends upon the skill of the speaker. The sermon should be practiced in advance, until all the details come readily to mind without notes. The sermon is more likely to be effective if the speaker enjoys himself in giving it. It is also helpful if he is a good actor, so that he can portray the emotions of his characters with his voice, and illustrate their actions with his gestures. When a story character speaks, it should not sound as though the narrator were speaking for him, but as though the character himself were speaking. The speaker should learn to sense the reactions of his congregation, so that he can know if their interest is being held, and if they are experiencing the desired emotions.

Depth of Content

The children's sermon should be simple without being shallow. Many of the great doctrines of the church can be taught through them. At the heart of the teaching program there should be the belief that every child needs to grow toward finding fullness of life through complete commitment to the Savior. For instance, the teaching should go beyond merely urging Junior to share his toys just for the sake of sharing. He should know that the real reason for sharing is because he belongs to Christ, and that this is Christ's way for him to live. Whereas such concepts as the life in Christ being a better one of peace and joy, now and forever, and the life without him being one of frustration, emptiness, and sadness, and the loss of eternal life, should not be preached to a child in adult terms, they can still be taught implicitly within the story-sermon.[1]

1 Story-sermons 3, 4, 7, 10, (among others) cite the joy of living for Christ. Story-sermon 22 tells of the promise of eternal life for Christians. Story-sermons 1, 6, 8, 12, 14, 26 (among others) cite the problems that come from the neglect of Christ.

When to Use Story-Sermons

Story-sermons, with visual aids to add interest, can be used almost any time children are gathered together for worship or religious instruction. In addition to the usual times on Sunday morning, they can be used in vacation Bible schools or junior youth fellowship services. For instance, story-sermon 22 is concerned with a basic problem of youth — the desire for popularity and the need for the self-esteem gained from recognition from others, and could be used as part of a youth program. In addition to the use of this story, material could be presented from real life, showing how some people are gloriously happy through expending themselves for others, and how others are miserable because they worry about what people think of them. Discussion questions could be asked about why young people showoff, why people need recognition from others, and how and why faith provides the answers to this problem.

Story-sermons 2, 9, 15, 18, 20, 24, and 25 are all taken from the Sermon on the Mount, and could be used as supplementary material in a study of this topic.

OBJECT LESSONS

How to Add Teaching Material to the Story-Sermons in This Book, in Adapting Them to Their Visual Applications.

A story can sometimes be made more forceful if a sermon is included in it as a part of the story. For instance, in story-sermon 11, one of Willie's hairs quotes Scripture and preaches to him. However, the sermon is only three sentences long and is a basic part of the plot. Willie must hear the hair's message if he is to reform.

Any story can have more teaching material added to it through the above method. If the story does not have a character in it to give a lecture (which will include the added teaching material) to the hero, such a character can be added. Many of the stories in this book will need the use of this method in adapting the story to the visual presentations. For instance, story-sermon 3, in its object lesson presentation, features a device for cripples to wear or use. In introducing this device, one could have Junior's father, in explaining what the Wobble, Wobble, Flops were, show Junior a crutch and say that nobody wants to have to use crutches because they are a sign of weak, helpless legs, and similarly the lack of practice will make a person weak and helpless in the area where he has failed to work.

How to Convert Any Children's Sermon into an Object Lesson Sermon

With a little thought it is possible to convert any children's sermon into an object lesson sermon. If the sermon is a story-sermon, it will be about an object, an animal, or a person. In the former cases, merely show the object or animal in actual, miniature, or pictorial form. If the story is about people, it will still have an abstract theme, such as "love," "greed," or "vanity," which can be pictured in a symbolic way. Thus a heart, a pig, and a peacock could symbolize these themes respectively. A children's story-sermon can be revised for the introduction of a symbolic object, by substituting a humanized object or animal to act the part of a person in the story; or by

83

allowing the object to come in contact with that person. For instance, a cloud of gloom could settle over a person's head, or a frown could be shown on his heart, or his head could change into that of a mule, or he could observe an animal or an object and learn from it. The story-sermons in this book are examples of these methods.

If a children's sermon is not in story form, one could display a symbolic object to represent the sermon theme, after altering the sermon to let this object play a prominent part in the sermon.

With enough thought, any children's sermon can be adapted into an object sermon. After thinking of a symbolic object adaptation for a sermon, it is often advisable to think further, and come up with something simpler or more appropriate than the initial idea.

How to Convert Object Lessons into Story Form

Object sermons can usually be improved by telling them in story form. To do this, think up some trouble or blessing that could logically (or illogically, if you want to let your imagination run wild) happen to that type of person, animal, or object, from success or failure in observing the sermon moral. If trouble results, the reformation of the character and a happy ending is optional.

Suitability of Objects

Discretion should be shown in the selection of objects for use in children's sermons. The object should emphasize the point of the story, rather than calling attention to itself. For instance, the first story in this book teaches the idea that selfishness brings unhappiness. The use of a grabby octopus enforces this concept. However if a person put a toy octopus in a bag, and then made a toy truck disappear and reappear in the bag with the octopus, the wrong things would be emphasized. The children would be more apt to remember the fact that a truck had magically disappeared, or that a octopus had a magic affinity for a truck, than to remember the lesson on selfishness. The flashy technique would call attention to itself, rather than being a servant of the moral. Magic and chemical object lessons can be of value, but the great danger in their use is that they so often appear to be showy effects with morals hitched to them as an afterthought.

A teaching object should be as simple as possible, as a rule. Complicated object lessons can be distracting.

A teaching object should represent an idea with a natural or a generally accepted relationship. For instance, the use of a pig to represent a dirty person is natural, because when one thinks of a pig he automatically thinks of a filthy sty. A glass of water that changes color chemically from clear to black would be a weaker such representation, because the congregation would never think of it as standing for dirt, unless the speaker so labeled it.

The Construction of Teaching Objects

Two-dimensional objects, or objects made of paper that folds or bends to take on a three-dimensional form, are preferable to solid objects because they are much easier to store. It is easier to use colored construction paper than it is to use paints in achieving colors. Colored paper also comes in gummed form. Felt pointed marking pens are the fastest way of outlining a paper surface. Latex house paint is a handy way to paint a large surface, as it dries rapidly and the brushes can be cleaned with water.

It is advisable to make objects as quickly and simple as possible. People in religious work usually have many demands on their time, so the making of intricate objects is not worth the investment in time. Simple objects are just as effective as elaborate ones. Simple rectangular and oval shapes can be put together to represent any object or animal. If their shape is not true enough to life to identify them, they can be labeled orally as they are introduced. A green oval or triangle on top of a thin, brown rectangle will do just as well to represent a tree as an intricately detailed model. An elephant can be made out of an oval, a half oval, and three rectangles. This principle is well illustrated by the drawings of two trees, an elephant, a giraffe, a pig, a dog, and a kangaroo. The geometric shapes can be held together with paper clips or brass paper fasteners. If holes are punched for the latter, motion can be given to animal legs.

One advantage in the use of simple geometric forms is that a lot of bright colors can be used, where they would not look right in a more lifelike representation. For instance, an elephant could be shown with a green leg, a red leg, a white body, a blue head, and an orange trunk. The bright colors would appeal to children.

85

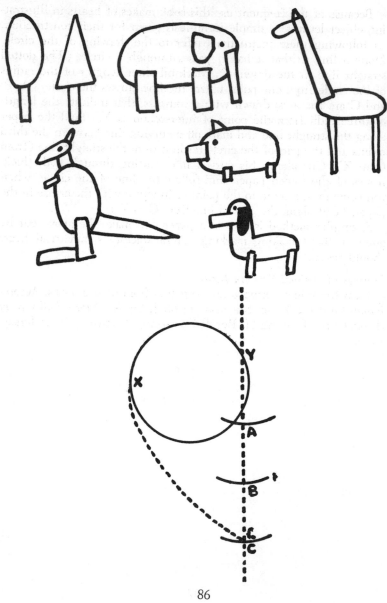

Because of the frequent use this book makes of hearts in illustrating object lessons, a simple formula is given for their construction. In following these instructions refer to the drawing of the circle. Draw a line so that it barely passes through a circle. (The dotted straight line in the drawing). Mark off three lengths of the radius of the circle from one point where the line crosses the circle. (A, B, and C are the arcs, drawn with a compass, that indicate the length of three radii from the point of intersection at Y.) Fold the paper along the straight line and mark off a curving line between the third radius and the part of the circle farthest from the straight line (from C to X). Cut along this curved line, cutting through both thicknesses of the folded paper, and follow the line of the circle, when you come to it, around to the point of juncture with the crease in the paper. (Cut along the curved line from C to Y.)

A simpler method is to fold a paper and make the above cut by guess, without making markings. A satisfactory symmetrical heart should result.

Sources of Animal Sermon Ideas

Ideas for animal sermons can be gotten from nature books, Aesop's *Fables,* and the Bible. See also: Jacob J. Sessler, *Story Talks from Animal Life,* Fleming H. Revell Company, Westwood, New Jersey, 1956.

PICTURE AND CHALK TALKS

Picture Talks

Many readers will not feel able to give chalk talks, but it is worth a try. Those who cannot master this art may draw the pictures in advance, with a felt point pen, on stiff 18″ by 24″ paper. Or they may get an artist friend to draw them. They will then be able to hold up the completed pictures during talks. In instances where chalk talk pictures are to be drawn in two stages of development, two completed drawings could be shown.

Chalk Talk Materials

CHALK — Lecturers chalk crayons are 3″ long, and either ½″ or 1″ square. The larger size is for shading with colors, while the smaller size is usually used for black outlining.

PAPER — 24″ x 36″ newsprint is the standard size. Some people prefer 36″ x 48″ paper, or this size cut down to 36″ x 40″. Many sheets of paper are used on a drawing board to provide a padded surface for drawing.

BALL BEARING CLIPS — Hold paper to easel. Clips that are 1⅜″ wide can be used for drawing boards ¼″ thick. Clips that are 2½″ wide will be needed for ½″ thick boards.

WHERE TO OBTAIN — These items may be obtained through an art or stationery store, or school art department. If necessary, a newspaper may help you find a source for a large size of newsprint.

EASELS — A simple easel can be made by placing a drawing board on top of a table and leaning the board against a wall. Rubber matting at the top and bottom of the board would protect table and wall surfaces. The easel can also lean against the flat back of a chair, placed on top of the table. Rubber matting under the chair will protect the table, and heavy books placed on it will keep it from slipping. A sturdy card table can be used for the table.

A piece of plastic or newspaper may be used to protect carpeting from falling chalk.

The drawing board should be the same width as the paper and

either the same height or 4" to 6" higher, for added height in drawing. The paper would be clipped to the top and bottom of the board. The backs of the corners of the board could be chiseled down to ¼" in width if you wish to use 1⅜" clips.

Here are instructions for making a simple table-top easel. A sturdy card table provides the portable bottom section. See the diagram.

Cut a piece of ½" x 2' x 3' plywood diagonally into two triangles (labeled "X" in the diagram). Take one of the triangles and measure 3" along the hypotenuse, from the angle made by the junction of the hypotenuse with the 2' side, and mark this point ("A" in the diagram). Draw a line between point A and the right angle of the triangle (point "B"). Cut along this line. (The dotted lines at the bottom of the triangles in the diagram indicate the wood that has been cut off.) Do this with the other triangle. These triangles are the sides of the easel.

A second ½" x 2' x 3' piece of plywood will become the drawing board. (This piece labeled "Y" in the diagram.) Fasten a ½" by 3"

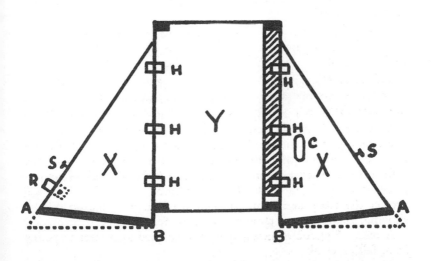

strip of plywood to one side of the drawing board with glue and screws. This will come down to within 3″ of the bottom of the board, and will allow the sides of the easel to stack in together when it is folded. (This strip is shown with diagonal shading lines on it in the diagram.)

Secure the sides to the drawing board with hinges, placing them as indicated. (Labeled "H" in the diagram.) Place the sides so they extend 3″ below the bottom of the easel.

Rubber matting should be stapled around the bottom of the easel sides to protect tables and give traction. (This matting is shown in black in the diagram.)

The black areas at the corners of the drawing board represent the areas that are chiseled from the back side, so that they can hold 1⅜″ ball bearing clips.

With the sides folded in, hold the easel so that its length extends out horizontally, and find the balance point. Make a "hand hole" in the side that folds outermost. (The long narrow oval, labeled "C" in the diagram represents a hand hole.) This will serve as a carrying handle.

A simple catch will hold the easel sides folded in. A thin strip of wood, 1½″ x 2½″, with a screw in its center, and fastened near the bottom of the side that folds innermost, will turn to lap over the outermost side. This strip is labeled "R" in the diagram. (The dotted lines show that part of it which lies behind the side.) The dot represents the screw.

LIGHTS — If lighting is needed for your easel, a desk lamp will do. It should have a flexible arm and a bullet-shaped metal shade to focus the light. The best place for it is on the floor in front of your easel. You can also use an adjustable clamp-on lamp fastened to the top of the easel. The lamp should be connected to an extension cord with a switch on it, so that the switch can be on the table where it is handy for you.

If an overhead lamp is used, it will be necessary to anchor the sides to keep the easel from tipping over frontwards. Fasten some screws to the easel sides near the bottom. (These screws are labeled "S" in the diagram.) Loop springs over these screws and fasten hooks into the loops in the other ends of the springs. These hooks can be made of thick wire obtained by cutting up a coat hanger. The hooks will hook under the bottom of the card table in the back. These devices can be easily slipped on and off.

BLACKBOARD — Paper can be saved by practicing drawings on a blackboard. Masonite painted with blackboard paint is the cheapest source of a blackboard.

Chalk Drawing

Anyone can use simple chalk drawings with children's sermons, no matter how poorly he draws. The important thing is to illustrate a point, not to show off drawing skill. If the speaker makes no pretense at being an artist, the crudest of drawings will still be effective. There is something fascinating about even a straight black line being drawn on a big sheet of white paper. Figures 9, 14, and 2 on this page are examples of extremely crude drawings illustrating story-sermons 9, 14, and 2. This level of artistic achievement could be achieved by any third grader, yet it is still effective.

If a picture is outlined lightly in advance with blue pencil, these lines will be invisible to a congregation.

Always stand to one side as you draw, so your audience can watch the picture progress. The key lines in a picture of a person are the lines of the mouth and eyes in the face. These should be drawn last, with the eyes usually drawn after the mouth, to give a climactic

finish. When shading in an area, thick, three-inch wide strokes should be made with the side of the chalk, splashing strokes sketchily over the area, rather than filling it in solid, as this adds speed to your drawing.

Talcum powder, applied in advance to the hands, will make them easier to clean. A dark-colored, moist cloth, kept on the table behind the easel, can be used to wipe most of the chalk off the hands, after the talk.

A helpful book is: Bert J. Griswold, *Crayon and Character*, Meigs Publishing Company, Indianapolis, Indiana, 1913.

Chalk Talk Supplies can be secured from Balda Art Service, Oshkosh, Wisconsin.

PUPPETRY

Two-Faced Hand Puppets

By adding an extra face to the back of a puppet's head and operating the puppet with both sides of the hand toward the audience, one can have a single puppet represent two people, or show two expressions. By painting one face a symbolic color, one can use this color as a teaching aid. Thus you could represent your puppet as being red in anger, or green with envy or illness. Also blue would show gloom, yellow would show cowardice or Midas-like love of gold, green would show growth, and purple would show royalty, or our sonship with God.

One may make a two-faced puppet by taping a cylinder of paper around the head of any hand puppet, such as are carried in the Christmas catalogues of large mail order companies or are in the catalogues of some non-denominational Sunday school supply publishing companies. One should paint large features on both sides of the paper. A smile on one side and a frown on the other will be useful for showing changes in emotion.

Light Bulb Hand Puppets

A light bulb puppet is made by removing the head from a standard hand puppet and sticking the bottom of a sixty-watt light bulb through the neck of the costume. The bulb is screwed into a light socket, on an extension cord, which is inside the costume. The thumb and index finger work the arms, while the lower three fingers clasp the socket and work the push-in type switch. Two white 4"x6" filing cards, glued into a 8¼" long strip are formed into a cylinder around the light bulb and held with paper clips. The top of the cylinder is narrower than the bottom to hold it on the bulb. A face is painted on the outside of the cylinder and additional features are painted on the inside, so that the expression of the face will change when the light is on.

The face can also change color, when the light is on, if a cylinder of typing paper, which has been colored with a felt point marking pen, is inserted inside the face cylinder. Instead of coloring this inner liner solidly, one might paint a cross or other symbol on it. However, this cross should shine through simpler facial features than those on the face cylinders described below.

This page shows a diagram of a face that changes from sadness (painted on the outside of the cylinder) to joy (painted on the inside) when the light bulb is turned on. the outside of the cylinder is painted a light flesh color, except the oval eye whites are left white. The shaded areas, in the bottom of the whites, are colored

with a mixture of flesh and red, and are on the *inside* of the face cylinder. Dotted lines around the eyes represent heavy black lines on the inside of the cylinder. On the outside of the cylinder, the eyebrows are black, the irises blue, the pupils black with white high-lights, the lines almost around the eyes are black, the nose is red with a black line around the bottom, and the frowning mouth (shown drawn with solid lines) is light red and *not* outlined with black. The lips on the inside of the cylinder (outlined with dotted lines) are bright red, the shaded mouth area is painted with a thick layer of black, and the teeth are white outlined with black.

The face that changes from a smile to a frown, diagramed on this page, is made along the same lines as the above one, with broken lines and shaded areas showing inside coloration and solid lines

showing outside coloration; and the same colors are used in comparable places, except the eyebrows are on the inside instead of the outside, black lines are added under the corners of the mouth on the inside, and there are no flesh-colored areas under the eyes on the inside of the cylinder.

The puppet costume should have cloth hands (so that your extended fingers push against the extremities of the hands), if you wish to lengthen the arms. The arms are lengthened by sewing longer cloth arms over the original ones, which are left the same length. The lengthened area is stuffed with cotton. The longer arms allow the puppet to reach two or more inches higher along its head.

A Glove Puppet

A glove puppet can be made from a very large, tan, cotton sock. See below for a diagram. Cut a slit (A) in the toe of the sock and sew a piece of red corduroy, reinforced with felt or interlon, around the cut edges of the sock so that a red mouth is formed (fig. 2). Large, round, cardboard eyes have brown irises, black pupils, white highlights, are rimmed with heavy black lines, and are glued to the sock. A pink cloth or felt tongue may be added. Stitches, on either side of where the thumb comes in the lower jaw, connecting the bottom of the jaw with the red lower mouth, will give better control of the mouth action.

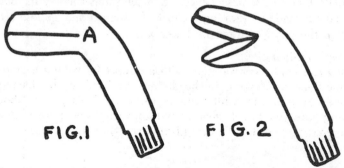

This glove puppet can be made into a dog by pinning on a black paper nose and long, hang-down ears. Put the ears on pointing upwards and it is a donkey. Make the ears short and pointed and add a body made of part of a sock with black spots on it, and it is a leopard. Add an oval pink nose with black nostrils and put the hand in the puppet upside down, with the thumb in the upper mouth and the four fingers in the jaw, and it is a pig. Remove nose and ears, and it is a worm. A bird is made by merely pinning paper wings to either side of the sock body. A skunk is made by sticking the regular head into a body made from a black sock. Part of the sock extends out as a tail. A white strip of cloth is sewn down the back of the body and tail. No legs are needed Shorten a paper bag and work the puppet inside the bag through a hole in the bottom and it is an oyster in its shell. Pin eight paper arms to the puppet body and it is an octopus. By sewing the toe of a sock in the shape of a trunk and pinning this over the upper mouth, you can make an elephant. Pin on appropriate paper tails, legs, ears, and it can form any number of animals.

The glove puppet can be made into a candle by placing a paper orange flame in its mouth and by pinning on a two-dimensional picture of a candle holder to its base. The candle is first shown to the audience with the lower jaw toward them, so that the eyes are out of sight. It can be made into a hammer by clenching the hand inside the puppet into a fist, and pinning on a two-dimensional picture of a hammer head to the head of the puppet. One's free hand should clasp the bottom of the puppet sleeve as though one were holding a hammer. The first is unclenched when the puppet moves its mouth. A cactus is made by pinning a paper "L" shaped and spinose cactus limb to the puppet under the lower jaw.

Puppet Manipulation

One can hold a conversation with a puppet by having it respond to questions by shaking its head "yes" or "no," or by having it whisper in your ear, while you repeat what it "says," as though making sure you heard what it said correctly. The puppet should be interesting to watch, by being full of short, lively motions.

SPECIAL DAY INDEX

Suggested material for special days is listed by story-sermon numbers.